The Pizza Puzzle

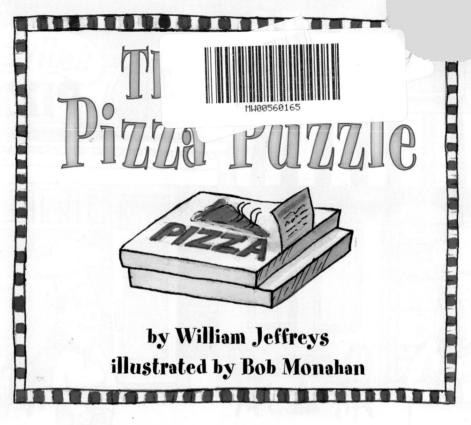

by William Jeffreys
illustrated by Bob Monahan

HOUGHTON MIFFLIN BOSTON

Printed in China

ISBN 10: 0-618-88699-0
ISBN 13: 978-0-618-88699-9

14 15 16 17 18 0940 21 20 19 18 17
4500648152

Pete made pizzas that were square.
He sold them at the summer fair.
The shop next door belonged to Pete's cousin.
Sally made round pizzas by the dozen.

Pete cut his square across.

He divided up the cheese and sauce.

Read • Think • Write How many slices does Pete cut?

Sally cut her pie. Is it the same?
She sliced across with excellent aim.

Read • Think • Write How many slices does Sally cut?

Roberto wanted to buy a slice.

He couldn't decide which one would be nice.

So he bought a slice from Pete.

Now the whole is incomplete.

Read • Think • Write What fraction of the pizza
is missing?

Roberto decided to have one more.
He bought one, then two, three, and four.

Read • Think • Write What fraction of Sally's pizza
is missing?

Roberto wanted to be fair
So he bought three more squares.
He shared them with his friend.
Sally and Pete both sold four slices in the end.

Read • Think • Write Who has more pizza slices left?

7

The Better Slice

Show

Look at pages 3 and 4. Draw a picture of the 2 different pizzas. Show how each pizza is cut.

Share

Look at pages 5 and 6. Tell what fraction of the pizza is left.

Write

Evaluate Look at page 7. Write what fraction of each pizza is missing.